THE NEW BIRTH

-a study of irresistible grace-

OTHER BOOKS
BY
JOHN G. REISINGER

Abraham's Four Seeds
But I Say Unto You
Chosen In Eternity
Christ, Lord and Lawgiver Over the Church
Grace
Our Sovereign God
Tablets of Stone
The Sovereignty of God in Prayer
The Sovereignty of God in Providence
Total Depravity
What is the Christian Faith?

THE NEW BIRTH

-a study of irresistible grace-

John G. Reisinger

NEW COVENANT MEDIA

5317 Wye Creek Drive, Frederick, MD 21703-6938

Phone: 301-473-8781 or 800-376-4146 Fax: 301-473-5128
Website: www.soundofgracebooks.com
Email: info@soundofgracebooks.com

In this book, the author has placed certain words from Scriptural quotations in italics or bold print without individually marking each instance with such words as "italics mine." The reader should be aware, however, that these italics and bold print are not found in the original texts but are added by the author for reasons of emphasis and clarity.

THE NEW BIRTH

-a study of irresistible grace-

ISBN 1-928965-08-3

Requests for information should be addressed to:

New Covenant Media
5317 Wye Creek Drive
Frederick, MD 21703-6938

We want to begin our study of the new birth by looking at three texts of Scripture that speak to this vital subject. The first passage shows not only the absolute necessity of being born again, but also states that being born again is essential before one is able to even 'see' the kingdom of God. In other words, we must have *sight,* the *ability* to see, before we can actually *see.* It is important to remember that seeing does not give us sight but we see only because we have sight. The gift of spiritual sight is given to us in regeneration and we *see,* or believe, because we have been given spiritual *sight.*

> In reply Jesus declared, "I tell you the truth, no one can see the kingdom of God unless he is born again". (John 3:3 NIV)

The second text also shows that the new birth must first take place before faith in Christ is possible; we will work this out in detail later.

> (10) He was in the world, and though the world was made through him, the world did not recognize him. (11) He came to that which was his own, but his own did not receive him. (12) Yet to all who received him, to those who believed in his name, he gave the right to become children of God—(13) children born not of natural descent, nor of human decision or a husband's will, but born of God. (John 1:10-13 NIV)

The third text shows that man has no more power over the new birth than he has over the wind. Both the wind and the Holy Spirit 'blow' as they please. Everyone knows that man does not have the power to either make the wind blow or force it to stop blowing. However, many sincere Christians do not realize that the same thing is true of the Holy Spirit's work in regeneration. A sinner cannot cause the Holy Spirit to regenerate his dead heart nor can he stop that work when the Holy Spirit purposes to do it! That is exactly what Jesus meant in this verse.

> The wind blows wherever it pleases. You hear its sound, but you cannot tell where it comes from or where it is going. *So it is with everyone born of the Spirit* (John 3:8 NIV).

When studying the Scriptures it is often necessary to isolate different aspects of truth. However, we must never try to isolate them in personal experience. Justification and sanctification are two entirely different things, yet it is impossible to experience one without the other. Both are an integral part of becoming and being a Christian, but they must be isolated to be studied. This is also true of regeneration by the Holy Spirit and personal faith in Christ for forgiveness. Regeneration is an essential *part* of salvation but it is not to be equated with being saved. It is a misuse of the word *salvation* to limit it to just *one aspect* of being saved. Salvation has at least three different aspects.

1. A Christian is truly *saved* right now (Eph. 2:8, 9—"have been").

2. A Christian is in the *process* of *being saved* every day (I Cor. 1:18 "...us who are being saved...").

3. A Christian is waiting in hope to be *fully saved* in the future (Rom. 5:10 "...we *were* [past tense] reconciled to him...having been reconciled...shall be [future tense] saved..."). Notice there is a clear distinction between *reconciled* and *saved* even though both are essential parts of salvation.

Sadly, our generation has confused 'being saved' with 'being born again'. One of these, being saved, has to do with *benefits* and the other has to do with *power* or *life.* One is the work and act of the sinner; the other, the work and act of the Holy Spirit. Notice the following two texts that show this distinction.

> And brought them out, and said, Sirs, what must I do to be saved? And they said, [You must] Believe on the Lord Jesus Christ, and thou shalt be saved, and thy house. (Acts 16:30-31)

> Marvel not that I said unto thee, Ye must be born again. The wind bloweth where it listeth [pleases], and thou hearest the sound thereof, but canst not tell whence it cometh, and whither it goeth: so is every one that is born of the Spirit. (John 3:7-8)

Acts 16:31 is teaching the necessity of a sinner having faith in order to be saved. God does not repent for us. The sinner must repent and believe. These are the acts of men and not the acts of God. Faith and repentance are not vicarious. If you have a problem understanding the relationship of these two things, see our tract, "God's Part and Man's Part in Salvation."[1]

On the other hand, John 3:8 is referring to power and ability. The work of the Holy Spirit in regeneration is likened to the blowing of the wind. A sinner can no more command or stop the regenerating work of the Holy Spirit than he can make the wind blow or stop a tornado. This is why regeneration is sometimes called 'irresistible grace'.

Being born again and being saved are both essential. It is impossible to experience one without experiencing the other. The question is not one of time and sequence, that is, which is first and which is second, but rather one of cause and effect. Does our faith cause the new birth or does the new birth cause faith? The question, "Why does one person believe and become saved, while another rejects Christ and is lost?" will be answered differently according to our understanding of the nature of regeneration. In one case, we will attribute the cause of man's faith to his free will, and in the other case we will give the Holy Spirit the glory for *enabling* us, by regenerating us, to believe and be saved. Perhaps the following will help.

---

[1] Available from Sound of Grace, 5317 Wye Creek Drive, Frederick, MD 21703-6938

Being *saved*—Acts 16:31	**Being *born again*—John 3:3, 8**
Benefits	Life and power
our work—our faith essential	God's work—our faith not involved
Acts 16:30—"What must I do?"	John 3:7, 8—"What must I do?"
Answer—"you must believe"	*No answer! God must do something!*
Faith—an act of man	Regeneration—a sovereign act of God
God does not believe for us	God gives new heart—we believe
Receive benefits of salvation	Receive spiritual life and power
Acts 18:27	I Peter: 1:2–3; James 1:18

I. Everyone agrees that man needs to be radically changed.

The Bible is quite clear as to the necessity of the new birth. My friend, Doctor Berry frequently asked, "Do you know why Jesus said, 'you must be born again'?" And of course his answer was, "Because you must be born again." George Whitefield preached over two thousand times on John 3:3. When asked why he preached so often on being born again, he replied, "Because you must be born again."

All churches believe you must be born again, but they radically disagree on what it means and how it happens. The Roman Catholic, Lutheran, Episcopalian, and Church of Christ all believe this happens through baptism. This is why they believe baptism is essential to salvation. Even Sigmund Freud had a doctrine of the new birth. He called it "An abrupt change in the continuity of the growth of the personality." Boy meets girl – boy falls in love – boy radically changes life style – boy is born again. In America today we are told that over forty percent of our citizens have had a 'born again experience'. If this is true, it must be the kind that Freud talked about. Most of the misunderstanding of the true nature of regeneration grows out of a failure to see *why* the new birth is absolutely essential. One will never understand the *what* and the *how* until one clearly sees the *why*.

II. Why is regeneration, or the new birth, so essential?

The nature of God demands it. God cannot fellowship or approve of anything that is not perfect. No one can stand in His presence without a total absence of sin and a positive robe of righteousness. We are sinners by nature and practice, and a holy God has no choice but to reject us. We need a spiritual birth that changes us and makes us acceptable to God.

The nature of the sinner necessitates a new birth. To be happy in heaven a sinner needs a new nature. Heaven would be a hell to a sinner without a new nature. Even if all his guilt was pardoned and a righteous standing imputed to him, until he is given a new nature, he would hate heaven. A friend has two sons that were constantly trying to impress their father that they loved Jesus and wanted to go to heaven. One day, on the way home from church, he asked them if they knew what heaven was like. When they had no answer, he explained that in heaven they sing a lot, they pray a lot, and they worship a lot. One of the boys said, "It sounds a lot like a church service." The father said, "Yes, that is a good description." The other son said, "You mean it's even longer than our church service?" About that time I suspect that someone had changed his mind about going to heaven.

Actually, the sinner cannot even want to believe the gospel until he is first born from above. Some of the verses that speak of man's *cannots* were covered in the study of depravity[2]. Only one of them

---

[2] John G. Reisinger, *Total Depravity* (New Covenant Media, Frederick, Maryland, 2000)

will be reviewed here. A comparison of three texts will reveal why a man needs to be born spiritually before he can believe.

> But the natural man receiveth not the things of the Spirit of God: for they are foolishness unto him: neither can he know them, because they are spiritually discerned. (1 Cor. 2:14)
>
> Even the Spirit of truth; whom the world cannot receive, because it seeth him not, neither knoweth him: but ye know him; for he dwelleth with you, and shall be in you. (John 14:17)
>
> These be they who separate themselves, sensual, having not the Spirit. (Jude 19)

One cannot receive and believe something about which he knows nothing, and one cannot know something that is totally beyond his ability to apprehend. I Corinthians 2:14 specifically states that a lost man cannot (that is, he does not have the ability to) *understand* spiritual truth, and therefore it is impossible for him to believe that truth. John 14:17 shows why this terrible reality is true. The lost man can only experience what he can touch, taste, feel, smell, etc., and God is not known by physical senses, but through the Spirit. Jude 19 is one of the best descriptions of a lost man that you will find in all of the Word of God. A lost man is merely a natural man who is totally limited in experiences to what his natural instincts can teach him. The sum total of his knowledge and experience is that which he can learn through his physical senses. This is what 'sensual' means. They who worship God must do so in "spirit" as well as truth and the lost man does not have ability to receive spiritual truth. He has all of the attributes of physical life but does not have the Spirit and can know nothing of spiritual life. He needs to be born of the Spirit before he can see, hear, feel, or experience spiritual things.

Man 'died' spiritually in the garden when he sinned. The Holy Spirit, the spiritual life of God in man, left Adam and he died spiritually. Now man is merely a 'natural' man without the capacity to experience spiritual things. Regeneration is the Holy Spirit, or the life of God, coming back into the sinner and empowering him with spiritual life and ability.

As we mentioned, every church agrees on the necessity of the new birth but they differ greatly on *why* it is essential and *how* it takes place. It is impossible to understand the *why* without grasping the truth of total depravity and its effect of total spiritual inability.

III. Exactly what is the new birth?

First of all, *it is a literal implanting of life, as in conception, that gives real life.* It is the cause of life and is evidenced later in a birth taking place. We are using 'birth' to include conception and actual birth. The point is that we are talking about spiritual implanting by the Holy Spirit that gives spiritual life. Just as there is physical birth that gives physical life so spiritual birth gives spiritual life.

Secondly, *this birth is 'from above.'* God is the sole author of this birth. The same Greek word translated *again* in John 3:3 is translated *from above* in John 3:31. Now it is true that the new birth is 'second' in that it is after the first birth—first physical then spiritual. However, the emphasis in the Scripture is not on the secondness of the birth but rather its *source.* It is from above us. It is not from *within* us; it is not from *outside* of us or *around* us; it is from above. It is a life giving birth from God that comes down to us by His power. This new birth has nothing to do with heredity, education, environment, culture, or church ceremonies; it comes directly from God alone.

Thirdly, *it is 'new' in the sense of RE-generation.* It is the sovereign implanting of life in the place of death. Two of the words which are used in the New Testament to describe the new birth or regeneration are *born* and *begotten*. They convey the fact of giving life through birth, Other words used are *regeneration* and *renewing*. These words show that life is put back into a place where it once was but where there is now only death. The Holy Ghost regenerates our hearts in the same sense that we regenerate a dead battery. Another phrase is *quickening* or *making alive;* "you hath He *quickened* who were *dead* in trespasses and sin" (Eph. 2:1). Regeneration is a "raising up," and bringing into being a "new creation." We could say, "The Holy Spirit brings dead sinners out of the grave of death, and resurrects the dead to life." Again, it is the idea of giving life to replace death. The new birth is literally a spiritual resurrection out of the spiritual death of sin. What Genesis 1:26, 27 was to physical creation, the new birth is to spiritual creation.

Comparing Genesis 5:1–3 with James 1:18 will help us to understand this by providing a picture of the nature and effect of regeneration.

> (1) This is the book of the generations of Adam. In the day that God created man, in the likeness of God [that likeness was not physical but a moral, rational, volitional likeness] made he him; (2) Male and female created he them; and blessed them, and called their name Adam, in the day when they were created. (3) And Adam lived an hundred and thirty years, and begat a son in his own likeness, after his image; and called his name Seth: (Gen. 5:1–3)

> Of his own will begat he us with the word of truth, that we should be a kind of firstfruits of his creatures. (James 1:18)

God *created* a son in "his own likeness" and Adam *begat* a son in "his own likeness." What does that mean? In both cases it means there is a definite *likeness* between the father and the child. Adam's son looked liked him, talked like him, walked like him because that son was Adam's true offspring. That son bore the physical image of his father. God created a child who had God's nature and bore God's spiritual image. That child was a physical creation, but he was also a spiritual being with a nature that saw and appreciated God in all of his works. Just as Adam's child was his true offspring and bore the physical image of his father, so Adam, at his creation, bore the spiritual image God. However, that original likeness to God was forever lost when Adam sinned. Regeneration is God 'begetting' one anew in his image and making him his eternal spiritual child.

The first man, Adam, was created in the likeness and image of God. After Adam sinned, he begat a son in his own likeness, after his image. James tells us that Christians have been begotten by God. Ever since Adam fell both God and men have been begetting true children in their own respective likeness and image. The children begotten, in both cases, share their father's life, bear his image, looks, nature, appetites, etc. In other words, through physical conception one acquires physical life and bears the nature and likeness of his human father, and through spiritual conception one acquires spiritual life and bears the nature and likeness of his spiritual Father, even God himself. In both cases there is true life, true birth, and in both cases the child born is the true offspring of its parent. The Christian is God's *child* (John 1:12). We are God's *seed* (Isa. 53:10; I John 3:8). Just as Adam communicated to his posterity, in physical birth and life, his looks, appetites, habits, motivation, and image in physical conception, just so God implants spiritual life and communicates His nature, likeness, motivation, and desires in His seed and they become a "new creation" by spiritual birth.

In James 1:18 we read, "Of his [God's] own will **begat** he us with the word of truth…." Christians are called sons of God. Just as Adam begat a son in his own likeness by procreation, so in regeneration God begets children in his own image from among sinners. He communicates to the "begotten ones" his likeness, his spiritual looks, and his desires. His children bear his image. They are truly God's offspring and bear God's likeness.

Now obviously the first question that one ought to face and seriously consider is this: **Have I been born of God?** One may use a physical birth certificate as proof of birth but one cannot use either a birth or baptismal certificate to prove any divine pedigree! We should ask ourselves: **Do I bear the image of God?** Am I a true Christian? Have I been born again? Do I have spiritual life?

When we are truly born of God we bear God's spiritual image just as surely as we bear the physical image of our natural parents. We are "like God" simply because we are his true children. This should be evident in the way we think and live. Christians disagree about many ideas, nonetheless, there are *some things that are true of every Christian who ever lived or will live.* Let me explain. Some churches do not believe in mixed bathing. Many Christians do not believe that you can smoke and go to heaven. Other Christians believe that women ought not to wear makeup or cut their hair. (Why do preachers always pick on the women?) There are Christians who believe, and do not believe, all kinds of tenets. There was a man on the radio preaching against "loving the world." He was not doing half bad until he decided to clearly explain what God meant by "worldly." He said, "Now any fool who is honest with the Bible knows that God is talking about playing baseball." He then went into a tirade against baseball. One may smile, but I would suspect that any given church may have some ideas that are just as strange.

I repeat, I know that Christians disagree on many things, but I still insist that there are some things that are true of every Christian who ever lived. It does not matter if he is ten years old or one hundred years old; whether his face is yellow, red, black, or white; whether he lived in the fifth century or the twentieth century; nor what his cultural or denominational background is or was. When a person is born of God there are some things that simply must accompany his conversion.

Let me illustrate. I had the unforgettable privilege of visiting the mission fields in Africa. Once I was preaching in a place where four different tribes with different dialects were in attendance. There were four different translators. It took an hour to preach a fifteen-minute sermon. Several times I became so engrossed in observing the different faces as the different translators spoke that I forgot what had been said. I had never seen any of those people before that day, but I could have gone through the entire congregation of about two-hundred and fifty people and without a single mistake, pointed to any person and identified the tribe to which that particular person belonged. How? Each person had a tribal mark cut into his face. When they were seven years old slashes were cut into their faces which left welts or scars. The number and direction or slant of the slashes was different in each case. You may have seen pictures of this in missionary meetings. Each tribe had its own mark. When a child is born into that tribe he is marked so that no matter where he goes he bears the tribal marks of his birth.

My friend, I assure you that the same thing is true of "God's tribe." Every Christian carries the tribal marks written in him by the Holy Spirit in regeneration. There are some distinguishing tribal marks on the people of God. When the Spirit of God brings the new birth he always writes the proof of his work in the heart and experience of every "begotten one." I John sets forth nine tribal marks, we have only listed four of them, which are true of every child of God. We may disagree about many facets of doctrine and practice, but every Christian wants to please God. He loves the revealed law of God and is committed to keeping it with all of his heart because it is the law of his heavenly Father and his Savior (I John 2:3, 4). If a person does not love the brethren he ought to doubt his salvation (I John 3:13–16). Why is John so emphatic? Because the new birth communicates the nature of God to His offspring. This is one of the ways to test one's conversion.

A friend of mine from years past was a fine lawyer who worked as a District Attorney for some time. A young lady came to him and accused a certain man of being the father of her baby. The man denied it and refused to marry her or do anything to help financially. At that time it was difficult to prove in court who the father was if the mother had slept with more than one man. Five men testified that they had slept with this girl within the time frame of when the girl had become pregnant. It seemed impossible to prove that the accused man was really the father. When the baby was born it had a very strange looking forehead. Instead of going straight up, the baby's forehead went back at about a forty-five degree angle. My lawyer friend had the mother sit where the jury could clearly see the baby's strange forehead. The accused man also had a strange forehead. In fact, his forehead was identical to the baby's. It also went back at a forty-five degree angle. The jury listened to all five men testify that they had slept with the girl. They listened to all of the technical, legal and medical arguments. They looked at the baby and they looked at the man and said, "You are guilty." They knew that man was that child's father because the father's physical image was stamped in the child. My friend, the same is true in the spiritual realm. The Father's image is stamped in every one of his children. Do you and I bear the marks of the image of God in our hearts and lives? Do we exhibit the proof of the work of the Holy Ghost in the way we think and act? Can you and I prove our divine pedigree? Can we prove that we have been regenerated? Have we been born of God? Someone has said, "If there was a law that forbid being and acting like a Christian, would your life furnish enough evidence for you to be convicted?"

I must digress for just a moment and insist that regeneration is not merely a theological doctrine about which to argue. It is a spiritual experience that is essential to true conversion! God, by his power, works and writes his very nature in our hearts and lives, and he always leaves "living proof." I fear some reformed people preach their own election. They think that understanding and talking about sovereign grace is the same thing as experiencing it. Being born again is not something *you believe,* it is something that you *personally experience.* You do not look at either your birth or baptismal certificate to see if you are part of the elect of God. Do not examine your denominational creed or your knowledge of the doctrines of grace to discover your election. Honestly examine your heart and life to see whether the Holy Ghost of God has given you spiritual life. Have you been spiritually and powerfully drawn to know, love and worship God Himself? That is the vital question.

This is what Jesus meant in John 6:44, 45. Too often verse 44 is used to prove 'total inability' [and it clearly does so] and verse 45 is ignored. John 6:44 and 6:45 must never be separated, either in our theology or our experience. Look carefully at the verses beginning with verse 44:

"No man can come to me, except the Father which hath sent me draw him…" In John 6:37, Jesus has just taught the doctrine of election. The Jews started to murmur at him. In essence He responded, You want to murmur at what I said. I'll really give you something to chew on. He then hit them with the doctrine of total depravity. "No man **can come** to me, **except the Father … draw him …"** (verse 44). Jesus does not stop there. He goes on to declare the truth of irresistible grace in verse 45. "It is written in the prophets. And they shall **be all taught of God. Every man** therefore that hath heard, and hath learned of the Father, **cometh unto me."** Notice the comparison in these two verses. John 6:44 says, *"No* man *can* come," and John 6:45 says, *"every* man who learns of the Father …*comes* to me." Drawing, hearing, and learning in these verses all refer to the same thing. Whatever "drawing by the Father" means in verse 44, the same thing is meant by "learned of the Father" in verse 45. Verse 44 is teaching inability. *"No* man *can* …*unless* …" Verse 45 is teaching effectual calling. *"Every* man *does* … *when* …" Verse 44 is affirming total inability and verse 45 is showing that regeneration brings men to Christ in spite of that depravity.

Every man who "hears" or "learns of the Father" will always, without exception come to Christ in faith, and no sinner ever will come, apart from the special regenerating work of the Holy Spirit. The new birth from God is a work that always produces saving faith and salvation. However, I repeat, we are talking about an experience and not just an abstract doctrine over which we argue. I ask you once more, Are you a Christian? Have you been born again? Or I could ask, Do you bear the marks, the pedigree, the tribal marks of the work of the Holy Ghost in your life? Regeneration is nothing less than the giving of spiritual life to a dead sinner. It is literally "being born of God."

IV. How does the new birth take place?

How is a man born of God? *First of all, it is not produced by baptism.* Neither the sprinkling of a child nor the immersion of an adult can regenerate a dead heart. Even if immersed by the apostle Paul, or sprinkled as a child by John Calvin (or both) one still must be 'born again'. Baptism, in any form, can neither wash away sin nor create a new heart.

There are two texts of Scripture which I think should settle the question of baptismal regeneration forever. "For though ye have ten thousand instructors in Christ, yet have ye not many fathers: for in Christ Jesus I have **begotten you** through the gospel" (I Cor. 4:15). Paul is here addressing people who have been begotten by the gospel through his ministry. He was their spiritual father. He was the only person who could say, "You are, under God's blessing, one of my converts." However, the apostle also says the following to the very same individuals: "I thank God that I **baptized none of you…"** (I Cor. 1:14). Do you see the logic of the two statements? If a man is regenerated or begotten by baptism it would be impossible for Paul to say, "I did not *baptize any of you* even though I have *begotten* you." If you put these two verses together, they prove beyond any doubt that baptism can have nothing at all to do with regeneration. If baptism is essential, or in any way contributes, to the new birth, then Paul could not have begotten converts without baptizing them. His argument and statements would be self-contradictory. The hymn writer was correct: "What can wash away my sin? Nothing but the blood of Jesus." Water, whether it is a few drops on our head as a child or a full tank into which we are immersed as an adult, cannot get into our heart where the change has to take place.

A missionary told of witnessing for many years to a Moslem friend. She was soon to go home and would not be returning because of ill health. She earnestly pleaded with God for one more opportunity to witness the gospel to her friend. One day she saw the Moslem woman start down the path to the sacred river to bathe. The missionary quickly put some clothes in a box, tied the box tight shut, and went down to the river and began dipping the box in the river. Her Moslem friend asked her what she was doing and she replied that she was washing her clothes. Her friend smiled and said, "They will never get clean because the water cannot get inside to where the dirt is." The missionary asked, "Do you believe that water in which you are bathing can get into your heart where the sin is and wash it clean?"

Secondly, the new birth is not dependent upon church sacraments. Partaking of the Lord's table, no matter how regularly, cannot give one a new heart. Paul forever put the death knell to the foolish notion that church sacraments can give spiritual life.

> But God forbid that I should glory, save in the cross of our Lord Jesus Christ, by whom the world is crucified unto me, and I unto the world. For in Christ Jesus neither circumcision availeth any thing, nor uncircumcision, but a *new creature.* (Gal. 6:14-15)

We may substitute baptism, or anything else, for circumcision in these verses and not change the teaching of these verses. The new creation is regeneration by the Holy Ghost. That is all a poor sinner needs, but he vitally needs that great work.

Thirdly, being born again has nothing whatsoever to do with human authority. Dr. Billy Graham may have personally put his hand on your head and told you that you are a Christian. That does not make you a child of God. That does not prove that you are born of God.

Fourthly, the new birth is not merely a correct knowledge of theology. Some current Calvinists are reviving an old heresy. It is called 'doctrinal regeneration'. They associate true salvation with a clear knowledge of Calvinistic theology. Some of these people imply that John Calvin is going to stand at heaven's door and examine you on your knowledge of the 'five points' (they call this the gospel) to see whether you get in or not. Not so, beloved! The five points are not the gospel. The gospel is, "Believe on the Lord Jesus Christ and thou shalt be saved." The five points are what makes the gospel work. Election never saved a single soul, but it does make certain that some will be saved.

Lastly, being born again has nothing to do with a man's so-called free will. Many people balk at this point. Look again at John 1:12, 13, and carefully examine the relationship of the two verses.

> (12) But as many as received him, to them gave he power [or authority] to become the children of God, even to them that believe on his name: [notice the sentence does not end here] (13) Which **were** born, not of blood, nor of the will of the flesh, nor of **the will of man,** but of God.

These Scriptures emphatically, categorically, and specifically state that we are *"not* born of the *will of man."* We are *"born of God."* Verse 12 tells what one must do to be saved. He must willingly receive Christ. The promise is that one will become a child of God when he receives Christ. The verse is clear. The tense of the verbs in these two verses is of utmost importance. John did *not* say that all who receive him, *will be,* as a result of believing, born of God. This would make faith to be the cause of the new birth. No, John said just the opposite. The people who receive Christ do so only because they *have been* (past tense) born of God. Their spiritual birth, given sovereignly by God, caused their act of faith. Verse 13 is not giving the *result* of verse 12, but rather the *cause.* Verse 13 tells exactly who the people are, in verse 12, that received Christ. The people in verse 12 willingly received Christ only because they *were* (past tense "had been") *born of God.* Do not mix up a *would be consequence* with a *had been certainty.* Every man who is born of God (v. 13) will always gladly receive Christ (v. 12). Receiving Christ (v. 12) is the certain result of being born of God (v. 13).

I John 5:1 teaches the same. "Whosoever that believeth that Jesus is the Christ *is* (already) born of God." John does not say that one *will be* born of God if he believes, but rather, if one believes it proves that he has been born of God. Faith is the **fruit** of being born again and not the **cause.** Some may say that I am just quibbling over words and say, "You cannot prove that from this text of Scripture." I am sorry, but the text can mean nothing else. This point may be proven by comparing I John 5:1 with I John 2:29. The identical construction is used but the subject is "doing righteousness" instead of being born again. The text: "...everyone that doeth righteousness is born of him." Is it just quibbling over words to insist that no one is born of God *because* he does righteousness? Do you not agree that we *do* righteousness only after, and only because, we *have been* born of God? We clearly know which is the cause and which is the effect in this verse. No one believes that "doing righteousness" *causes* one to born of God. That destroys the gospel. The same identical truth is set forth in I John 5:1. Our faith does not cause the new birth, but, like "doing righteousness," our faith is a living proof that we *have been* born of God. To deny this clear fact is to destroy the biblical doctrine of regeneration. A man cannot born (active voice) himself, but he must be born (passive voice) from above.

When an evangelist announces that he is going to preach on, What you must do to be born again, proceed with caution. This man is not making the biblical distinction between being saved and being born again. He may preach biblically about how to be saved, but certainly not about how to be born again. He will probably say, "You had nothing to do with your first birth, but you have everything to do with your second birth." He is dead wrong! You had no more to do with your second, or spiritual birth, than you did with you first, or physical birth. There is no denying that a sinner must willingly repent and believe the gospel in order to be saved, however, we are talking about born again. We are insisting that only God can give the power, or the "want to," that enables one to repent and believe.

Sometimes I like to tease people in order to stimulate them to think. When people argue for the doctrine of man's free will, I often say to them, "I do not discuss the doctrine of free will with anybody who doesn't believe in eternal security." They usually say, "Who said anything about eternal security?" I look rather puzzled and ask, "You surely do not believe a sinner has a free will and also believe that a saint can never be lost?" They almost always reply emphatically, "Yes, I do." In pretended surprise, I ask, "Are you saying that a sinner has the will power to either accept or reject Christ?" When they affirm that they believe this, I ask, "Can a saint will, or choose, his way out of grace?" When they say "No," I reply, "Well, if the sinner has power to both accept and reject, but once he accepts, he can no longer choose to be lost, it sounds to me that you believe a sinner has twice as much will power as a saint. You are saying that we *lose part of the freedom of will that we supposedly had before we were saved."* The dialogue usually ends at this point. It is nonsense to hold to a doctrine that teaches that man loses half of his will power when he is converted. It is impossible to believe both free will and eternal security. They are self-contradictory.

The new birth is something that God does in us, without us. It is his sovereign work, but it always produces fruit in our lives. Let me try to illustrate this. Suppose that I was away from home for a speaking engagement and after the service my car would not start. When I turned the key in the ignition there was not even a buzz. I flipped the light switch and there was not even a flicker. I pressed the horn and there was not even a peep. Someone would probably say that he thought that my battery was dead. Suppose they were correct and the battery was indeed dead. I leave the car in the church parking lot and go off to bed. The next morning I once more try to start the car and the motor immediately turns over. There are three possible explanations of what happened. (1) The battery was not really dead, I just thought it was. (2) A miracle took place. (3) Somebody re-charged, or "regenerated," the battery.

Now just suppose the various parts of my car had the power of speech. Suppose, the evening before, I had said, "Lights, if you will only shine that will put life in the battery." Or, "Horn, if you will only blow that will put life in the battery." If my car could speak it would have replied, "If you put some life in the battery I guarantee you the horn will blow, the lights will shine, and the motor will start." So it is with the man who is dead in sin. His spiritual battery is dead. None of his facilities will work until he is regenerated. When God gives a sinner life, he will repent, believe, pray, etc. Appealing to a lost man's will as the source of power to save him is like appealing to the lights and the horn. It is *life* that the lost man needs just as the car battery needs life. The most powerful spiritual feat possible is the exercise of faith. It can move mountains. Does a dead man produce the spiritual power to perform the powerful act of faith, or does he do this because of regeneration and the gift of a new nature?

When I come back and found the battery working, I would assume that somebody had been fooling around underneath the hood. Wouldn't you? Some years ago, my wife and I took our son and daughter-in-law to a Bible conference. My son was a good "All-American" boy but we weren't really sure if he had been converted. He knew all of the right answers but did not seem to have a thirst after God. I preached four messages on the doctrine of total depravity. After the second message my son came up to me and said, "Dad, that's the first sermon I ever heard you preach. Something happened to me tonight. I think I got converted." He has not been the same since that night. He now exhibits the fruits of true conversion. I believe that night Somebody was fooling around under the hood. My son had heard me preach for twenty-two years, but that night he "heard the voice of Christ." That night he was regenerated and believed the gospel.

Have you ever witnessed to a person for years but they paid no attention to you? Then one day you see them reading a Bible and they show up at church. What had happened? Somebody was fooling around under the hood. You prayed for your children and instructed them in the word of God but it seemingly went in one ear and out the other. Then one day, like my son, they say to you, "Why didn't you tell me this before?" You smile and realize that someone was fooling around under the hood. The Holy Ghost has been charging a dead battery. That is what the Bible calls regeneration and this is what we need to see today. We do not need better buildings, preachers, or music programs. We need someone with the power to do something under the hood.

V. Being born again is a creative act of the Holy Spirit.

We must emphasize again that being born again has nothing to do with heredity. It has nothing to do with our parents or church sacraments, and it surely has nothing to with man's so-called free will. Free will is to spiritual life exactly what evolution is to physical life. It is a blatant denial of God's creative power. It amazes me that sincere Bible believers do not see this awful fact. It causes them to make injudicious statements. The following quotation from the Scofield Bible's footnote on John 3:3 is an illustration:

> *Regeneration*: (1) The *necessity* of the new birth grows out of the incapacity of the natural man to "see" or "enter into" the kingdom of God. However gifted, moral, or refined, the natural man is absolutely blind to spiritual truth and impotent to enter the kingdom; for he can neither obey, understand, nor please God (John iii.3, 5, 6; Psa. li.5; Jer. xvii.9; Mk. vi.21-23; 1Cor. ii.14; Rom. viii.7, 8; Eph. ii.3. See Mt. vi.33, *note*). (2) The new birth is not a reformation of the old nature (Rom. vi.5, *note*), but **a creative act of the holy Spirit** (John iii.5; i.12, 13; 2 Cor. v.17; Eph. ii.10; iv.24). (3) **The condition of the new birth is faith in Christ crucified** (John iii.14, 15; i.12, 13; Gal. iii.24). (4) Through the new birth the believer becomes a partaker of the divine nature and of the life of Christ Himself (Gal. Ii.20; Eph. ii.10; iv.24; Col. i.27; 1 Pet. i.23–25; 2 Pet. i.4; 1John v.10–12.[3]

How can a **"creative** act of the Holy Spirit" be **"conditioned"** in any sense whatsoever, and especially on something a poor sinner must do? That is like God saying, "I will create the world if you will agree to allow me to do so." Scofield confuses being

[3] *The First Scofield Reference Bible,* C.I. Scofield, ed., (Barbour and Company, Inc., Westwood, NJ, 1986), p. 1117

saved with being born again. See Volume 5, Issue 1 of *Sound of Grace*[4] for a detailed study of the difference between these two.

VI. The sinner is passive in regeneration.

In all the references to the new birth in the New Testament Scriptures, regardless of which word is used, the voice of the verb is always passive. No one ever birthed himself, or regenerated himself. The sinner is always passive and not active in regeneration. He does not *do* anything. Something is done *to* him, but nothing is done *by* him. As mentioned earlier, the sinner has no more to do with his second birth than he did with his first birth. You did not decide to be born spiritually any more than you decided to be born physically.

Again, we insist that we are not talking about time sequence, but cause/effect. The new birth and repentance/faith are simultaneous; however, regeneration makes faith possible and not vice versa. Lydia's conversion is a classic example.

> And a certain woman named Lydia, a seller of purple, of the city of Thyatira, which worshipped God, heard us: whose **heart the Lord opened,** that she attended unto the things which were spoken of Paul. (Acts 16:14)

Everyone agrees that Lydia must have heard, understood, and responded in personal faith to the gospel message of grace before she could be saved. The text clearly shows that all of these things happened. Lydia heard, understood, and responded—and that most willingly—to Paul's preaching. The question is this, What was it that enabled Lydia to respond in faith? Did she, with her own free will, open her own heart and invite Christ to save her? That is not what the text says. The text says, **"The Lord** opened [Lydia's heart so] that she attended unto the things which were spoken..." Lydia's response was made possible by God regenerating (opening) her heart. The sinner's heart must indeed be opened, but

---

[4] Available from Sound of Grace, 5317 Wye Creek Drive, Frederick, MD 21703-6938

a spiritually dead sinner cannot open his own dead heart. He bolts it shut with ignorance and fear. Only God himself can open a dead sinner's heart, and this he does for all of his elect. This is being born again. This is being made alive, or quickened (Eph. 2:1).

I am sure that some of my readers are saying, "You are preaching irresistible grace and I know the Bible clearly teaches that the sinner can resist the work of the Holy Spirit. What do you do with Acts 7:51, 52?"

> Ye **stiffnecked and uncircumcised in heart and ears**, ye do **always** resist the Holy Ghost: as your fathers did, so do ye. Which of the prophets have not your fathers persecuted? and they have slain them which shewed before of the coming of the Just One; of whom ye have been now the betrayers and murderers… (Acts 7:51, 52)

Pay particular attention to the words in bold type. There is no question that the text specifically declares that men can and do resist the Holy Spirit. In fact, the text says more than that, it uses the word *always*. I think every reader will agree that they have resisted the Holy Spirit in their past. Who among us did not laugh at the people who first witnessed to us the truth of the gospel? By nature, every sinner will not only resist the gospel, but he will *keep on resisting it*. The question is this: Why did every saved person decide to quit resisting and instead decide to repent and believe? Why is that word *always* not true of most of those who read this book? Again the text is clear. The people Peter was addressing were **stiff-necked and uncircumcised in heart and ears**, and do could nothing but resist. Every sinner will always resist as long as his heart and ears have not been circumcised. Regeneration is the Holy Spirit taking the resistance out of us and circumcising our heart and ears so that we want to believe. The verse does not refute irresistible grace but shows how essential irresistible grace is in true conversion.

One more concept is important in this text. The resistance spoken of in these verses concerns the voice of the Holy Spirit speaking *in the prophets*. Sinners can and do resist all of men's preaching and exhortations. My son totally resisted all my entreaties with him for twenty- two years. You may turn a deaf ear to the message when preached by men, but when that message is applied to the conscience directly by the Holy Spirit the resistance is removed. The internal work of the Holy Spirit in regeneration is quite different from the outward work of human agency. The former cannot be rejected, but the later can and is rejected by many.

The phrase *irresistible grace* turns some people off because they think of a steamroller rolling over a tube of toothpaste. That is not the irresistible grace of the Bible. We are not tubes of toothpaste. We are creatures with minds, hearts, and wills. The same mind, heart, and will that fervently resists the gospel is made willing in regeneration to stop resisting and sincerely repent and believe. Let me illustrate biblical regeneration. Two mothers were having a cup of tea and the one mother's son came down stairs neatly dressed, his hair neatly combed, and his shoes shined. As he went out the door whistling his mother said, "That really bugs me." The other mother asked, "What do you mean? I wish my son looked like that. He dresses like a slob." The first mother replied, "Oh, that is not what I mean. What really bugs me is that a blond head and a pair of blue eyes did in ten minutes what I could not do in sixteen years."

That is the kind of irresistible work that we are talking about. That boy did not have to dress neatly if he did not want to. From his mother's remarks we gather that she had tried, without success, to get him to change his appearance. Then one day an irresistible attraction made him want to change, and he did so immediately and most willingly. You did not have to receive Christ unless you really wanted to, but when the Spirit of God showed you your heart and then revealed the beauty and glory of the Son of God, you wanted to receive him with all of your being. Irresistible grace is nothing less than God taking the resistance out of us and making us "willing in the day of his power" (Psalm 110:3).

Man indeed needs to hear the gospel preached, but he also needs something more. He needs a new heart. The boy's mother gave him many correct and heartfelt instructions, but nothing worked until an irresistible force came along.

VII. The means God uses—his Word and the Holy Spirit.

Perhaps we should have added the word *normal* to the above heading. The classic text to show what we mean in the above statement is I Thess. 1:4, 5.

> Knowing, brethren beloved, your election of God. For our gospel came not unto you in word only, but also in power, and in the Holy Ghost, and in much assurance; as ye know what manner of men we were among you for your sake.

It is obvious that Paul had assurance that the people to whom he was writing were part of God's elect. How did Paul know this? It had nothing to do with their pedigrees or baptismal certificates. It was because of the effect the Word of God had upon them. It is important to note that the gospel always comes in words. It does not come in dreams and visions, nor in a baptistery or communion cup. The gospel comes in *words.* It comes in propositional form. It comes as written facts of history. The gospel tells us, in concrete words, exactly who Christ is, and what he has done. .

However, words by themselves are not enough—*even the words of God.* This is why Paul adds the word *also.* The gospel always comes in words but unless those words are attended with the power of the Holy Spirit they do not prevail in opening a sinner's heart. This is why we said the means that God [normally] uses are his Word and his Spirit.

Two things need to be said: (1) Many Scripture texts connect the Word of God with regeneration. However, (2) it would seem that regeneration may take place without the Word of God being applied to the mind and heart. Infant salvation would not be possible if the Word of God had to be the instrumental cause of regeneration. Having said both of these things, we can say that nearly every instance where regeneration is specifically mentioned it is always in connection with the Holy Spirit using the Word of God. Note the following instances:

> The **entrance of thy words** giveth light; it giveth understanding unto the simple. Ps 119:130 [This verse needs to be compared with 2 Cor. 4:4–6, "In whom the god of this world hath blinded the minds of them which believe not, lest the light of the glorious gospel of Christ, who is the image of God, should shine unto them. For we preach not ourselves, but Christ Jesus the Lord; and ourselves your servants for Jesus' sake. For God, who commanded the light to shine out of darkness, hath shined in our hearts, to give the light of the knowledge of the glory of God in the face of Jesus Christ."] Ps 119:130
>
> Of his own will **begat he us with the word of truth,** that we should be a kind of firstfruits of his creatures. James 1:18
>
> For though ye have ten thousand instructors in Christ, yet have ye not many fathers: for in Christ Jesus I have **begotten you through the gospel.** 1Cor. 4:15
>
> **Being born again,** not of corruptible seed, but of incorruptible, **by the word of God,** which liveth and abideth for ever. 1Pet. 1:23

These verses do not prove that the Word *must be* the instrumental cause of regeneration but they do show that it is the emphasis in all of these recorded instances of regeneration.

VIII. The new birth is great mystery—so is physical birth.

John 3:8 and I Peter 1:23–2:1 demonstrate the mystery of our subject. John tells us that being born again is as mysterious and sovereign as the blowing of the wind. Peter tells that the union of a man and woman that produces a new life is also a mystery. We need to look closely at Peter's words:

> Being born again, not of corruptible seed, but of incorruptible, by the word of God, which liveth and abideth for ever. For all flesh is as grass, and all the glory of man as the flower of grass. The grass withereth, and the flower thereof falleth away: But the word of the

> Lord endureth for ever. And this is the word which by the gospel is preached unto you. (1 Pet. 1:23-25)

Jesus told us that we must be born again, and Peter here tells us how that takes place. Verse 23 compares our spiritual birth to our physical birth. We were begotten when a seed from our father was planted in the ovum of our mother. That seed had the power to beget life itself. That seed produced a new creation. That which was not, you, "became" in the womb of your mother. You were begotten and then born of a seed but unfortunately that seed was a corruptible seed. All that seed could produce was a child that must die. No human seed has ever produced a child with everlasting life. When we were born of God we were begotten with the seed of God, and that seed in incorruptible. It produces children that have everlasting life. That seed is nothing less than the Word of God. As that word is eternal, so is everything that word begets.

Peter then compares our existence on this earth to that of a flower. All flesh is like the grass and the flower. You plant a seed, a few days later there is a stem and then a flower. Several more days and it dries up and blows away. Man is the same. Yesterday I was a little boy, today I am a grandfather, and tomorrow I will gone and no one will know I was here. However, the seed of God produces plants of grace that are a sweet smelling savor to God for all eternity because they will not wilt and die. When the Holy Spirit plants the seed of God in the ovum of a sinner's heart there is a new creation. We are truly "begotten of God" through His Word of truth and the power of the Holy Spirit.

IX. The Certain Evidences—John 3:8.

The passage we quoted in 1 Thess.1:4,5 goes on to show the radical change in those to whom the Holy Spirit has applied the Word in power. Look at verses 6–10:

> And ye became followers of us, and of the Lord, having received the word in much affliction, with joy of the Holy Ghost: So that ye were ensamples to all that believe in Macedonia and Achaia.

> For from you sounded out the word of the Lord not only in Macedonia and Achaia, but also in every place your faith to God-ward is spread abroad; so that we need not to speak any thing. For they themselves shew of us what manner of entering in we had unto you, and how ye turned to God from idols to serve the living and true God; And to wait for his Son from heaven, whom he raised from the dead, even Jesus, which delivered us from the wrath to come.

They faithfully "followed the Lord" even through times of great affliction. They were living examples of sovereign grace and witnessed their faith far and wide. They forsook their idols and turned completely to the true God, and were keenly looking for the second coming of Christ.

One of the Puritans said, "If you get soundly converted even your dog will know something happened to you." John 3:8 is emphatic about the absolute sovereignty of the wind's actions, however, the wind cannot blow without giving clear evidence of its work. The tree leaves move and the clothes on the line wave back and forth. Some of us have seen first hand evidence of the awesome power of a hurricane or a tornado. All of us have seen pictures on TV newscasts of a hurricane destroying a coastal town. The same thing is true spiritually. The Holy Spirit always leaves the marks of his work in the life of a true believer. Some of these marks that "accompany salvation" [Hebrews 6:9] are listed in 1 John. Look up each time John uses the words *we know* and you will have a partial list of proofs of the regenerating work of the Holy Spirit. Galatians 5:22–26 is another list of evidences that the Holy Spirit is "blowing" in a person's life.

X. Summary

The nature of God and of man requires that man must be radically changed in order to be acceptable to God. That radical change is described in Scripture as a new birth that God works in man, without the assistance of man. It is a creative act of the Holy Spirit. The evidences of this creative act are faith and repentance, which in turn produce other distinguishing marks. The new birth is God's work, wrought in man through the Holy Spirit, which results in true spiritual life that is evident by the manner of life of the converted sinner.